What Happens When You Flush?

Kelli Hicks

rourkeeducationalmedia.com

Scan for Related Titles and Teacher Resources

Before & After Reading Activities

Level: **F**   Word Count: **218 Words**

100th word: *hole* page 10

Teaching Focus:
Concepts of Print: One to One Correspondence- Point to each word as you read.

Before Reading:

Building Academic Vocabulary and Background Knowledge
Before reading a book, it is important to set the stage for your child or student by using pre-reading strategies. This will help them develop their vocabulary, increase their reading comprehension, and make connections across the curriculum.
1. *Read the title and look at the cover. Let's make predictions about what this book will be about.*
2. *Take a picture walk by talking about the pictures/photographs in the book. Implant the vocabulary as you take the picture walk. Be sure to talk about the text features such as headings, the Table of Contents, glossary, bolded words, captions, charts/ diagrams, or index.*
3. *Have students read the first page of text with you then have students read the remaining text.*
4. *Strategy Talk – use to assist students while reading.*
   - *Get your mouth ready*
   - *Look at the picture*
   - *Think…does it make sense*
   - *Think…does it look right*
   - *Think…does it sound right*
   - *Chunk it – by looking for a part you know*
5. *Read it again.*
6. *After reading the book complete the activities below.*

Content Area Vocabulary
Use glossary words in a sentence.

float
gravity
sewer
stopper
tank
vacuum

After Reading:

Comprehension and Extension Activity
After reading the book, work on the following questions with your child or students in order to check their level of reading comprehension and content mastery.
1. *How do toilets fill back up with water? (Asking questions)*
2. *Where does the waste from the toilet go? (Summarize)*
3. *What do you do after you use the toilet? (Text to self connection)*
4. *What are the two main parts of a toilet? (Summarize)*

Extension Activity
With an adult, look at the toilet in your home. Have an adult lift the lid off the tank and look inside. What do you see? Look at the diagram in the book and locate all the parts in the tank. Now flush the toilet and look inside the tank. What do you notice? Where does the water go? How does it fill back up? When the tank is filling up what is happening inside the toilet bowl?

Table of Contents

What's That Sound?

Do you hear that flushing sound? Everybody uses a toilet, but have you ever thought about how it works? What makes that sound?

A Simple Machine

A toilet is really a simple machine. Most toilets use **gravity** to move water in and out.

Some toilets use little or no water. These toilets use the waste collected to help the environment.

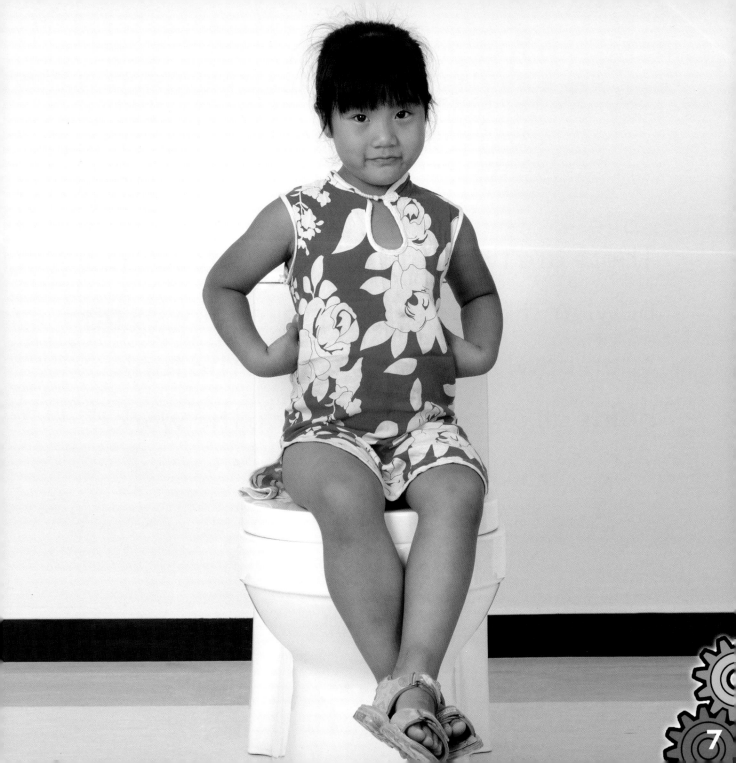

There are two main parts to a toilet: the bowl and the **tank**. The toilet bowl is an open bowl that holds water. The tank holds all of the parts that do the work.

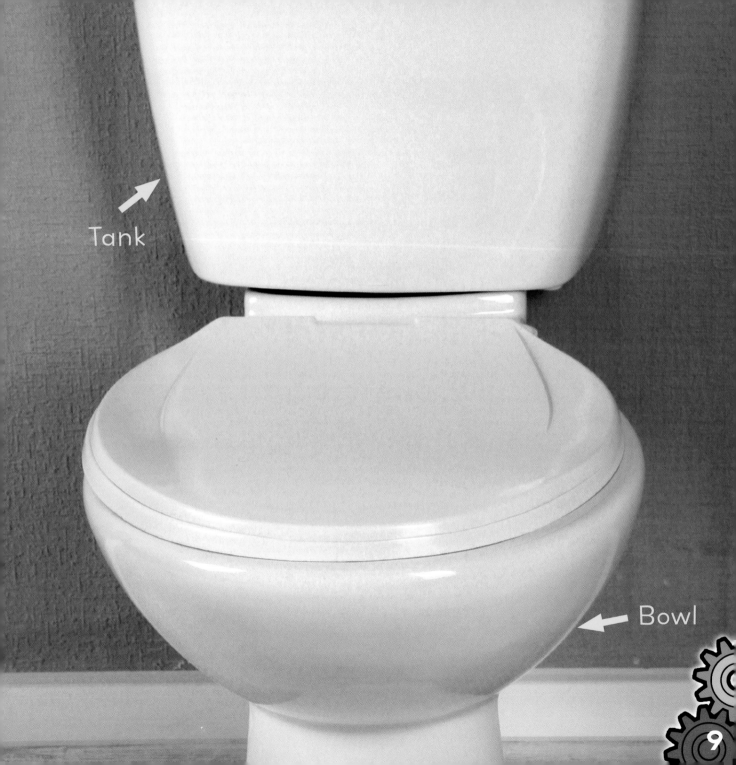

Tank

Bowl

9

The Flush

When you push down on the toilet's handle, a chain in the tank lifts a rubber **stopper** called the flapper. Clean water rushes down through a hole and into the bowl.

The Flushing Cycle

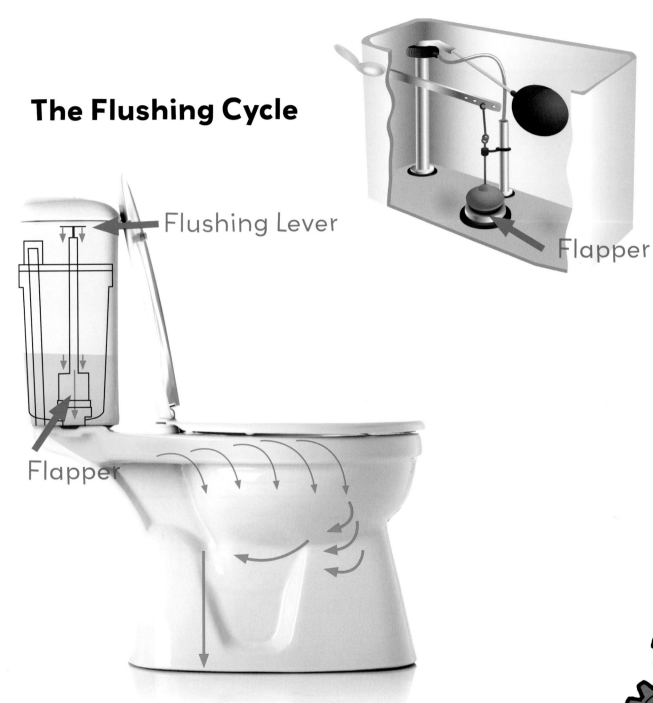

Flushing Lever

Flapper

Flapper

Water enters the bowl through small holes under the rim.

Water fills the bowl and helps clean it.

At the same time, dirty water goes down a pipe at the bottom of the bowl. The quickly moving water and the pipe work like a **vacuum**. The waste is pulled down into the **sewer**.

Water needs to move quickly to remove waste from the bowl. Fast-moving water creates airflow and air pressure, which pulls the waste and dirty water out of the bowl.

The Refill

When the tank is empty, the flapper covers the drain hole again. The tank refills with clean water for the next flush.

The Refilling Cycle

Flushing Lever

Flapper

It takes three seconds for one flush to push dirty water out of the bowl and less than one minute to refill the tank.

A **float** in the tank rises with the water level.

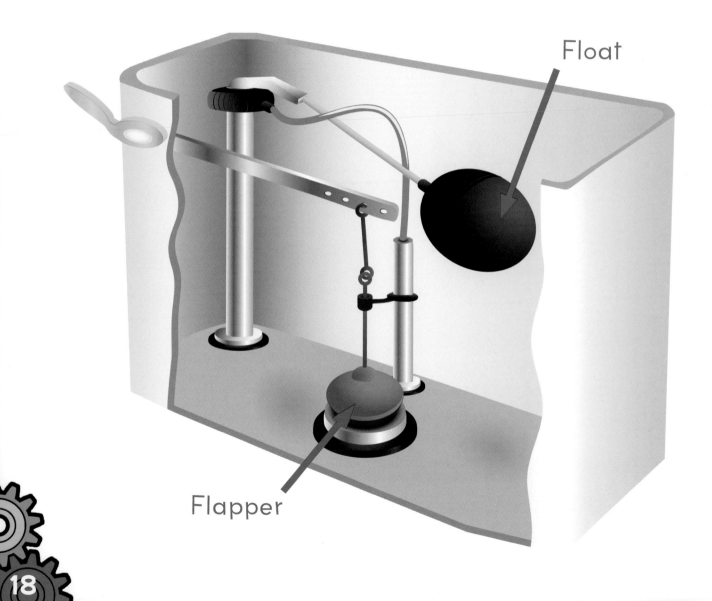

Float

Flapper

When it reaches the top, the tank is full, and the water flow stops.

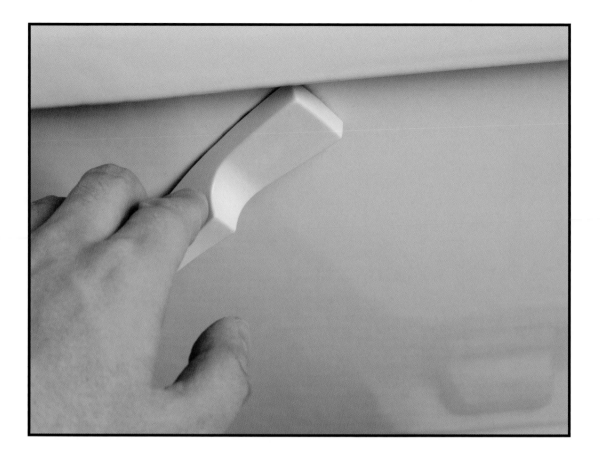

The cycle repeats with every push of the handle. Did you remember to flush?

Photo Glossary

 **float** (FLOHT): A float rests on the top of a tank of water. It goes up or down as water enters or exits the tank.

 **gravity** (GRAV-uh-tee): Gravity is the force that pulls objects down.

 **sewer** (SOO-ur): An underground pipe that carries away liquid and solid waste is called a sewer.

 **stopper** (STOP-ur): A stopper is a piece of rubber or plastic that seals an opening.

 **tank** (TANGK): This is a large container that holds liquid.

 **vacuum** (VAK-yoom): When all the air has been emptied from a sealed space, a vacuum is created. In a toilet, a vacuum helps move waste through the pipes.

Index

Websites to Visit

aggie-horticulture.tamu.edu/kindergarden/kidscompost/kid1.html

www.physics4kids.com/files/motion_gravity.html

www.inventors-trunk.com/fun-toilet-facts.html

About the Author

Kelli Hicks is a teacher and author who lives in Tampa, Florida with her husband, two kids, and golden retriever. Knowing how a toilet works, she is able to fix it whenever necessary. In her free time, she can usually be found at the soccer field, enjoying a piece of chocolate, or reading in a big comfy chair.

Meet The Author!
www.meetREMauthors.com

© 2015 Rourke Educational Media

www.rourkeeducationalmedia.com

PHOTO CREDITS: Cover © DamianPalus; title page © Peopleimages.com; page 5 © Andrey-Kuzmin; page 7 © Photobee; page 9 © africa-studio.com; page 11, 17, 18, 22, 23 © Nicola Spasenski, Designua; page 12, 13 © delihayat; page 15, 23 © scholes1; page 19 © c-photo; page 20 © Kovalchuk Oleksandr; page 21 © Nanette Gvebe; page 22 © roadragedsb; page 23 © serezniy

Edited by: Jill Sherman

Cover and Interior design by: Jen Thomas

Library of Congress PCN Data

What Happens When You Flush?/ Kelli Hicks
(How It Works)
ISBN (hard cover)(alk. paper) 978-1-62717-648-4
ISBN (soft cover) 978-1-62717-770-2
ISBN (e-Book) 978-1-62717-890-7
Library of Congress Control Number: 2014934240

Printed in the United States of America, North Mankato, Minnesota

Also Available as:

ROURKE'S
e-Books